W9-BLR-433
R02084 56948

DEER *and* ELK

A whitetail fawn.

DEER *and* ELK

by Dorothy Hinshaw Patent
photographs by William Muñoz

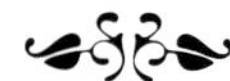

CLARION BOOKS
New York

ACKNOWLEDGMENTS

The author and photographer wish to thank Aransas National Wildlife Refuge, Texas; Homosassa Springs State Wildlife Park, Florida; Lowry Park Zoo, Tampa, Florida; Lee Metcalf National Wildlife Refuge, Montana; National Bison Range, Montana; and Yellowstone National Park, Wyoming. Special thanks go to Dr. Daniel Pletscher, University of Montana, for reading and commenting on the manuscript.

Clarion Books
a Houghton Mifflin Company imprint
215 Park Avenue South, New York, NY 10003

Type is 14 pt. Bembo
Book design by Carol Goldenberg

Printed in Italy.

Library of Congress Cataloging-in-Publication Data
Patent, Dorothy Hinshaw.
Deer and elk / by Dorothy Hinshaw Patent ; photographs by William Muñoz.
p. cm.
ISBN 0-395-52003-7
1. Deer—North America — Juvenile literature. 2. Elk — North America — Juvenile literature. 3. Wildlife management — North America — Juvenile literature. I. Muñoz, William. II. Title.
QL737.U55P36 1994
599.73′57—dc20 93-25894
CIP

NWI 10 9 8 7 6 5 4 3 2

To Janet Chenery

Contents

A mule deer doe.

Chapter One

Graceful Survivors

As the car turns the corner, its headlights illuminate the image of a deer by the road. The animal's slim legs look fragile as it stands facing the barbed wire fence bordering the field. Then, as the people in the car watch, the animal springs effortlessly from a standing position, easily clearing the fence, walks slowly away across the pasture, and disappears into the darkness.

Deer are among the most common wild animals in America today. Even city dwellers may get to see them in wooded parks near the outskirts or in suburban fields and yards, especially around dusk and dawn. Like a few other wild animals such as raccoons and sparrows, deer have found ways of continuing to survive, even where people

Deer are most often seen at dawn or dusk.

have taken over the land. These graceful animals are a common subject for children's stories. The elk, a large deer that brings to mind the Wild West, is also widely known. But most people actually know little about these animals, for popular stories like *Bambi* give a mistaken impression of how these beautiful creatures really live.

The Deer Family

Members of the deer family, called by scientists Cervidae, are familiar animals in much of the world. Forty-five different species are found in northern Africa, Asia, Europe, and South America. White-tailed deer, mule deer, elk, moose, and caribou (reindeer) are the North American Cervidae.

Cervids are plant eaters that live in a great variety of habitats. Some prefer forests, while others thrive in the desert. The caribou's home is the cold, barren arctic tundra, while the Chinese water deer lives among the reeds and rushes that border the rivers in the Yangtze Basin of China and Korea.

Most deer are brown, gray, red, or yellowish in color, with a lighter-colored rump patch and pale underparts. The young of many species have spotted coats that help camouflage them in the dappled light of the forest or in the tall grass. Some species, such as the handsome Axis deer, keep their spots even after they grow up, at least for part of the year. Male deer are usually larger than females.

A caribou bull.

A mule deer fawn with its spotted coat.

The words used to describe cervids can be confusing. Female deer are called does (pronounced *doze*), while female elk (as well as moose and caribou) are dubbed cows. Male deer are bucks, while male elk are called bulls. A deer gives birth to a fawn, while an elk cow has a calf.

The Antlered Animals ❧

The most striking trait of cervids is their antlers. Only Chinese water deer lack these impressive bony growths that rise from the skulls of the males. In just one species — caribou — females also carry antlers.

People often confuse antlers with horns, but the two structures are really quite different. Horns are grown by animals in the family Bovidae, such as cattle and antelope, and are permanent, bony growths of the skull covered with a protective sheath. Horns grow slowly from the base throughout the animal's lifetime. Antlers, on the other hand, are temporary bony structures that regrow each year and have no outer layer when fully developed. They grow at the tips instead of from the base. In most deer species, the antlers have a complicated branched shape. Each year, until the animal gets old, the antlers get larger. However, the number of branches on antlers is not necessarily equal to the animal's age. Antlers can be huge — those of a bull

A bull moose.

This young whitetail buck is beginning to grow antlers.

The antlers of this bull elk are in velvet.

moose may weigh 67 pounds (30 kilograms) and have a spread of more than 6 feet (1.85 meters) from tip to tip.

When a male cervid is born, his skull is just like that of a female fawn. But as he gets older, a pair of bony stalks called pedicles grow upward from his skull on each side of the head. The pedicles end just under the skin.

The antlers grow from the pedicles, their bony cores covered by a furry layer of skin called the velvet. The velvet is filled with blood vessels that provide nourishment to the growing antlers. It also contains nerve endings so the deer can sense when the antlers touch something. These nerves and the thickness of the velvet help protect the antlers as they develop. Blood vessels within the soft bone also help nourish them.

When the antlers have finished growing, the blood supply to the velvet is cut off at the level of the pedicles. The velvet dries up, and the buck rubs it off on tree trunks and bushes, leaving hard, shiny bone. The vessels inside the antlers also shrivel, so the mature antlers are actually dead, insensitive bony growths attached to the skull. The antlers remain in place for varying lengths of time, depending on the species of cervid. In mule and white-tailed deer, antlers are shed in autumn or early winter, while elk keep theirs until early spring. In the springtime, small animals like mice and ground squirrels chew on shed antlers on the ground to obtain needed minerals.

Antlers are important to the mating success of male cervids. During the breeding season, the antlers are full grown. The bucks and bulls are on the lookout for females and for one another. When two males meet, they challenge each other. Generally, the larger the buck, the more impressive the antlers. A buck with a big rack of antlers has a better chance of winning over one with smaller antlers, so he is more likely to keep females for breeding. Usually, just the sight of a huge rack will deter a smaller male. But if a fight does ensue, the buck with the larger antlers is more likely to win.

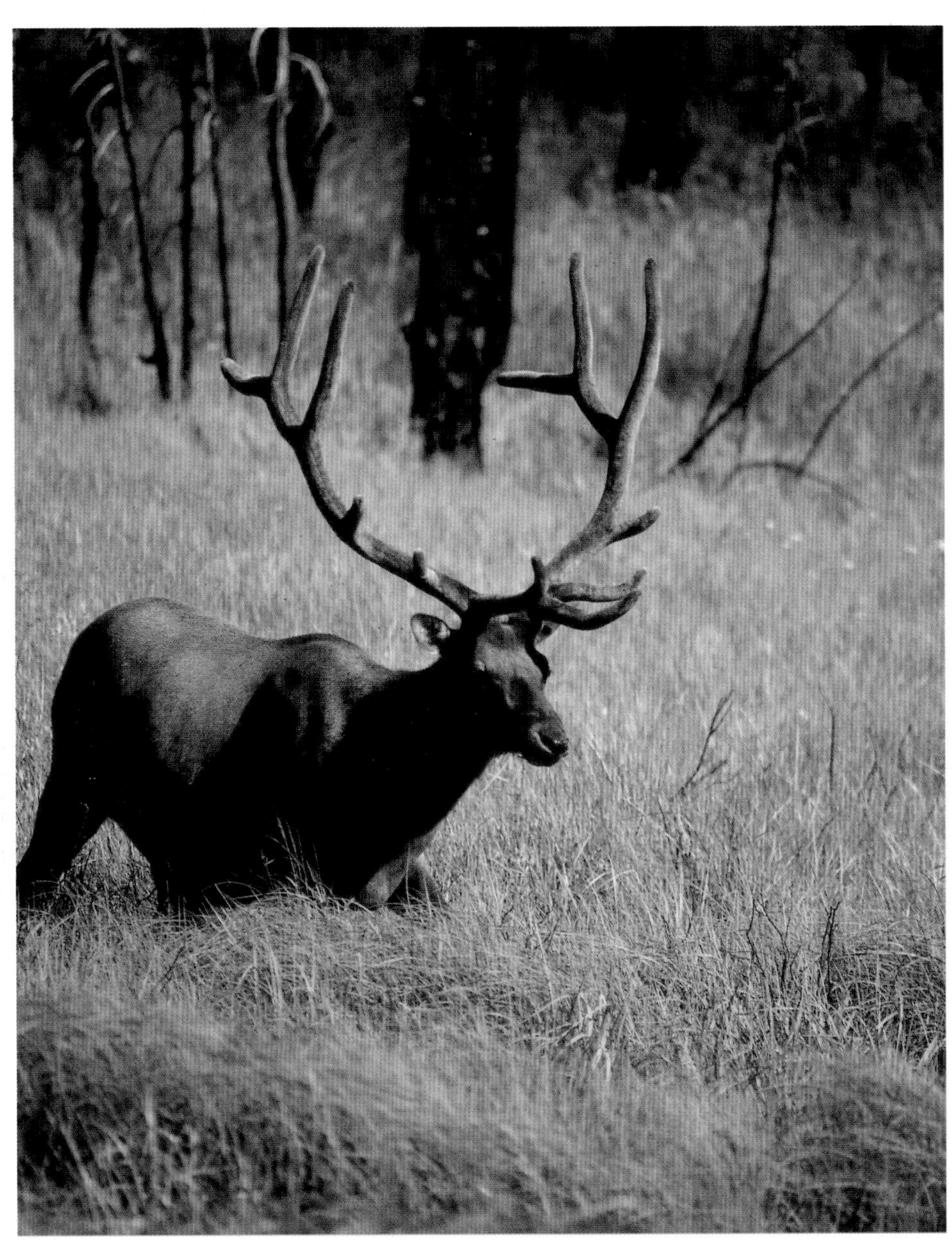

A bull elk with big antlers.

Many things about cervids — in both their physical appearance and their behavior — can be explained by their role in nature as prey animals. Deer eat plants, and other animals eat deer. In North America, members of the deer family can fall prey to mountain lions, bobcats, wolves, coyotes, grizzly bears, black bears, and humans.

A deer's head shows several adaptations to help the animal avoid becoming prey to powerful hunters. Its eyes are large and are located at the sides of its head, enabling the deer to see almost completely around itself, even while grazing. Its vision straight ahead isn't very good by human standards. Scientists have discovered that the fallow deer (found mostly in Asia) can't make out shapes beyond a distance of about 100 feet (31 meters). But it can spot the tiniest movement even as far away as 1,000 feet (310 meters). Being able to detect movement, which can mean a stalking predator, is more important to a deer than being able to recognize shapes.

Deer have large ears that can turn independently this way and that to focus on sounds from any direction. The deer's sense of smell is very sharp, so it can identify danger that is approaching from upwind. Their sense of smell is also important for social reasons, for cervids have scent glands that are used to communicate with other deer.

The coyote sometimes preys on elk calves and deer.

These whitetails are alert to any danger.

Most deer are designed for fast running, and they can escape predators if they have enough warning. Members of the deer family stand on the tips of their third and fourth toes for speed. Hard, tough hooves are protective coverings over these toes. Their legs are long, slim, and lightweight. The muscles that power them are mostly bunched up into the body. Deer can leap high to clear obstacles in their paths, and their graceful agility allows them to zigzag their way through trees or up rocky slopes when they need to make an escape. Most members of the deer family have light-colored rump patches that flash behind them as they flee, warning other deer of danger.

Deer have cloven hooves, meaning there are two toes in the hoof.

Deer are well camouflaged — there is one at the center of this photo.

A deer's color helps camouflage it in the forest or brushland. Even the skittish whitetail may simply freeze like a statue if a person walks by along a woodland path. The deer can see the human, but the person may be completely unaware that wild animals are nearby.

Though deer rely on flight and camouflage most of the time to protect themselves from enemies, they are far from helpless. When a doe hears her threatened fawn bleat, she comes running to its aid and can sometimes chase off a hungry coyote or a young mountain lion. Deer can strike out with their sharp hooves and cause serious injury, and bucks have been known to kill potential predators, including human hunters, with their antlers. Picnickers should stay away from tame deer that haunt picnic areas. Every year, many people in the United States are injured and several are actually killed by deer aggressively protecting themselves or their young.

How Deer Eat ❧

All members of the deer family are plant eaters. Some cervids prefer to feed on the leaves, shoots, twigs, flowers, and fruit of trees, herbs, and shrubs. This feeding is called browsing. Others are more likely to graze on grasses. Cervids that spend most of their time browsing tend to live somewhat solitary lives. Their food appears in patches, where there is enough for only one or a few animals to eat. Food is also usually found in protected places like within the woods, where the animals can be concealed from enemies. Grazers are exposed in open areas, where predators can see them. But their food is also abundant, with grassy meadows extending for long distances. By living in groups, grazing members of the deer family can help one another look out for danger — many eyes, ears, and noses are more likely to notice an enemy than those of just one lone animal.

Along with bovids, giraffes, camels, pronghorns, and mouse deer, cervids are ruminants. That means they have a

Grazers like elk tend to live in herds.

After feeding, ruminants like this mule deer retire to a protected place to chew their food more thoroughly.

special kind of stomach with several chambers that is very efficient at digesting plant food. Plants are largely made up of a tough material called cellulose. Cellulose is very difficult to break down chemically. Only a few worms, slugs, and snails are able to digest cellulose. Instead, ruminants provide a home in their complex stomachs for tiny bacteria and single-celled protozoa that can break cellulose down chemically.

Ruminants feed by eating rapidly, nipping off plants and

swallowing them quickly. In this way, they can take in a large amount of food in a short time, limiting their exposure to predators. After feeding, the animals retire to protected places, where they regurgitate their food a mouthful at a time and chew it more thoroughly. Then they reswallow it, and the microorganisms in their stomachs digest it. The microorganisms utilize some of the nutrients in the food for their own growth and multiplication. The ruminant animal absorbs the rest into its own body. In addition, some of the microorganisms are carried with the food remnants into the small intestine, where they themselves are also digested and help nourish their host. But since the microorganisms keep reproducing, there are always plenty of them present in the stomach.

Chapter Two

White-Tailed Deer

The white-tailed deer (*Odocoileus virginianus*) is familiar to most Americans, for it lives across most of North America, from coast to coast in southern Canada and the Pacific Northwest and from north to south along the eastern seaboard. The whitetail is absent in most of California, Nevada, and Utah. This highly successful animal is the most widely distributed hooved animal on the continent.

Recognizing a Whitetail

The whitetail's giveaway is its namesake — a foot-long tail with brilliant white underside fur. When a whitetail is busy grazing or resting, its tail hangs down, showing white just around the edges. But if the animal becomes alarmed, up

A whitetail buck.

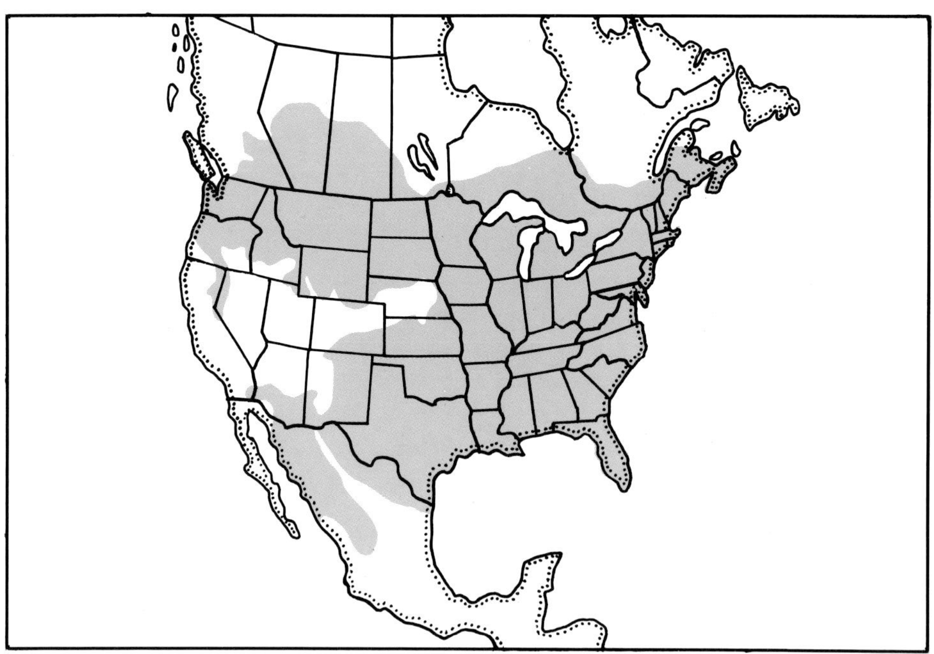

Whitetail deer distribution.

goes the tail, unveiling both the white underside and the white rump patch below. The deer waves its tail back and forth as it bounds away from danger, flagging a warning to any other deer in view.

During the summer, a whitetail's coat is a golden reddish brown. In fall and winter, its more grayish fur blends in well with dead grass and the muted colors of the forest. Both summer and winter, the belly fur is white, and there are white markings on the face and neck.

Whitetails vary greatly in size over their wide range. A large northern whitetail buck can weigh as much as 400

Whitetails wave their tails back and forth while fleeing.
Alert white-tailed deer.

pounds (180 kilograms). In the southern states, the animals are smaller, with a buck weighing in at around 220 pounds (100 kilograms). The smallest of all American deer is actually a variety of whitetail, the endangered Key deer of Florida. Bucks of these tiny creatures are only about 2 feet tall (62 centimeters) and weigh at most 80 pounds (36 kilograms).

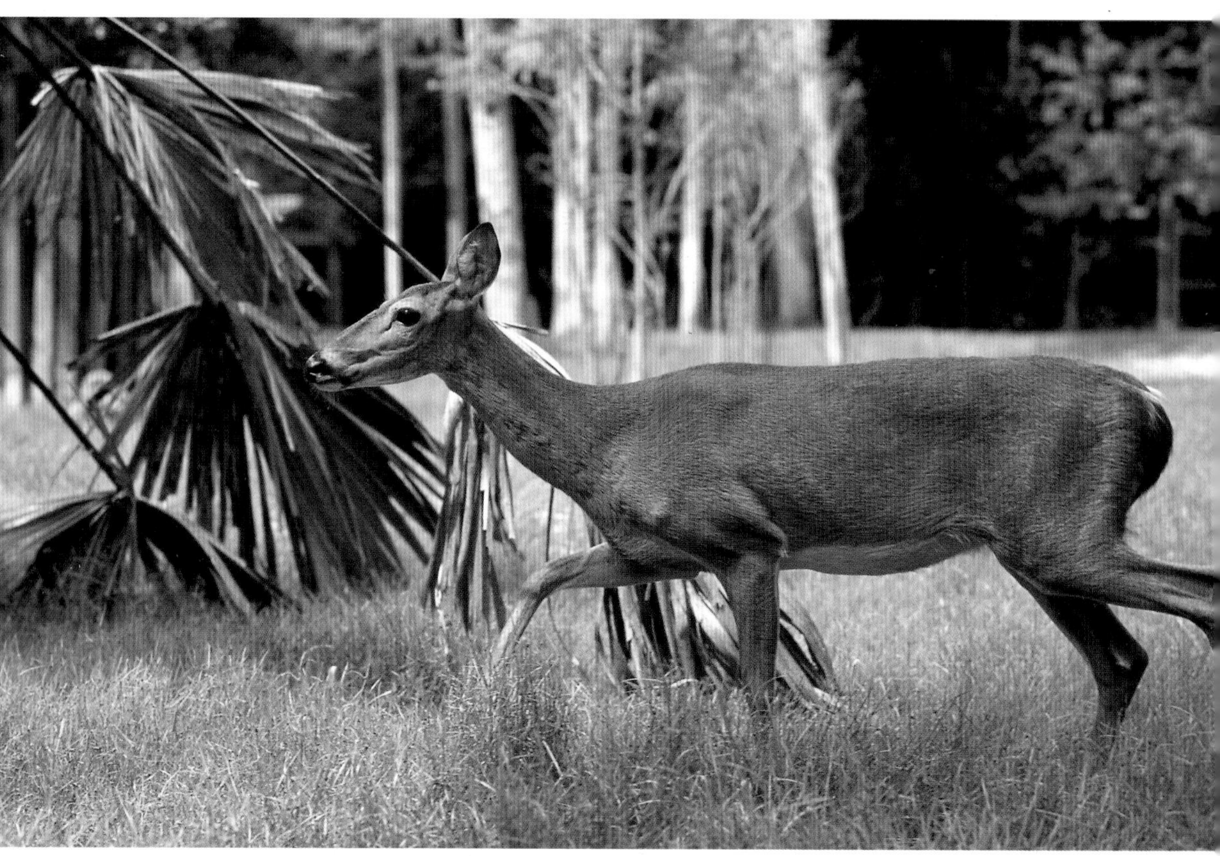

Whitetails in Florida are smaller and more delicate than in the north.

A key to the whitetail's success is its adaptability. But given a choice, these animals prefer to live around the edges of habitats, such as creek beds and along the borders of meadows. These places provide food and water and are close to the cover of trees for escaping from predators. Dense forests and wide open spaces are not likely to harbor large populations of whitetails.

Whitetails prefer to browse on the shoots, leaves, buds, and bark of woody plants. But they also enjoy acorns and domesticated grains such as corn and soybeans, which can get them into trouble with farmers. In some farmlands, crop plants make up half the diet of whitetails.

In spring and early summer, whitetails eat the tender new growth of broad-leaved plants that may grow among the meadow grasses and in the forest. Where other food is scarce, these adaptable animals will feed on grass, too.

Most of the year, whitetails live alone or in small groups. But during the winter, large numbers of whitetails may gather where shelter and food are plentiful. This is especially true in northern areas, where snowfall can be heavy. By "yarding up" together, the deer tramp down the snow into trails so they don't have to struggle through deep drifts. Both food and shelter are nearby, so the deer are protected from bad weather and don't need to waste energy searching

Whitetails can have trouble moving through the snow in winter.

for something to eat. Because their metabolism slows down during the winter, the animals require less food than at other times of year.

Whitetails breed during fall and winter. In autumn, the deer tend to gather in large groups in open areas, especially at night. By then, antlers are full grown and the velvet has been shed. The bucks begin to spar with one another. At first, the sparring matches may last only a few seconds. One buck will lower his rack in front of another. Often, the second buck accepts the challenge and the two click their antlers together with little pushing and shoving. Between bouts, the bucks may feed. As the season progresses, the sparring matches become gradually more intense. In this way, the bucks get to know one another's strength without serious battles. By the time the does are ready for mating, the bucks are all well aware of who is strongest. During the

A whitetail buck.

actual mating period, the largest, healthiest bucks are most likely to mate. Few real battles over possession of does take place, since the bucks know which of them would win.

The time of mating varies greatly from north to south. In northern Michigan, for example, 80 to 90 percent of mating takes place in November. In the southern part of the state, breeding stretches into December. And in southern states like Mississippi, mating can be spread out over a four-month period. In the tropics, whitetails may breed at any time of year.

New Life

Whitetail fawns are born in late spring or early summer, commonly in late May or early June. In northern portions of their range, as many as 90 percent of the fawns may be

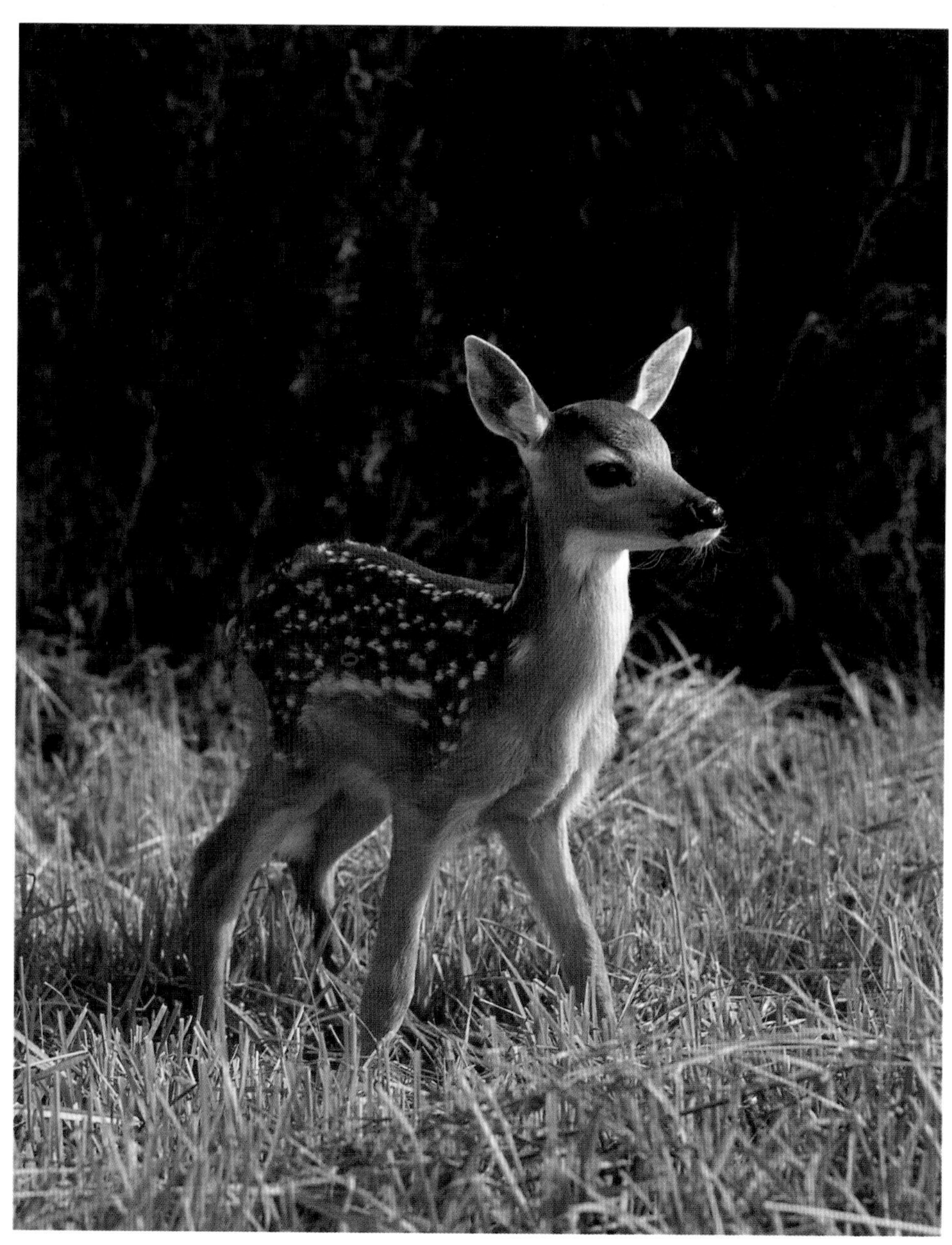

A whitetail fawn.

born within a one-week period. Does usually give birth to twins, and triplets are common. A young doe is capable of breeding her first fall and thus may give birth to a single fawn when she is only a year old, although most does do not mate until they are eighteen months old. Because they can breed at such a young age and usually bear twins, whitetails can increase their numbers very rapidly when conditions are favorable.

As the time for birthing approaches, the doe begins to defend a territory of from ten to twenty acres in size. There she gives birth and lives with her fawn or fawns for about a month. Each year, she is likely to use the same fawning territory. Her daughters fawn nearby, in territories that may overlap that of their mother.

After the fawns are born, the mother licks them clean and eats the afterbirth. She cleans up all signs of the birth, minimizing the odors that could alert predators to a good meal. Healthy fawns weigh about five pounds each. Before they stand up, the fawns nurse on their mother's special rich colostrum milk. The colostrum, which is secreted right after birth in all mammals, is high in fats and protein, and it contains antibodies that will protect the fawns from disease until their own immune systems become active. Within a half hour of birth, the fawns are standing. They can walk short distances within a few hours.

From then on, the doe hides her fawns when she leaves to feed. She separates the fawns from each other. That way, if a predator succeeds in catching one, the other is likely to survive. The spotted offspring are well camouflaged, and they have little scent. As long as they remain completely still, they have a good chance of being safe. But even a slight movement can alert a nearby predator. If a predator does find a fawn and tries to attack, the fawn will bleat loudly and try to run away. The mother responds immediately to her fawn's cries for help. She may fight off the predator if it is small, or she may try to distract a large predator and get it to chase her instead of attacking the fawn. Her fleet

The doe is always watching for danger to her fawn.

The fawn stays motionless in a protected place while its mother is away.

hooves are likely to outdistance a chasing predator as she leads it away from her offspring. A doe returns to her fawns for nursing only two or three times a day and may be gone for as long as twelve hours at a time. After feeding, she leads her fawns to new, clean places to bed down.

Caution on the part of the doe is essential for the fawns' survival. In the Adirondack Mountains of northern New York, for example, about 30 percent of the fawns are killed by coyotes and black bears each year, mostly during the first month of life.

Growing Up

Fawns grow rapidly on a diet of their mother's rich milk. They double their weight during their first two weeks and get stronger every day. Throughout the summer, does with fawns tend to keep to themselves, using the cover of the forest and brush to remain as inconspicuous as possible. Meanwhile, the rest of the whitetails — bucks and females without fawns — may gather in small groups.

All the deer concentrate their energies on feeding during late spring and summer. Bucks need to build up reserves for the strenuous autumn mating season, called the rut. Nursing does must eat plenty to nourish their own bodies and those of their fawns. The does spend up to 70 percent of their time eating. For the fawns, which begin sampling plants when they are just a few days old, putting on weight is critical for their survival in the coming winter. By the

Whitetails, like this one in Texas, may feed on grass in the early spring.

time they are about five weeks of age, fawns need both mother's milk and plant food. By ten or twelve weeks, most fawns do little or no nursing.

As they get older and stronger, fawns are less secretive. Instead of lying hidden in the brush whenever they aren't feeding, the fawns romp and play with one another, chasing and running circles around their mother. They buck and kick and leap, building up their strength and agility and learning about their bodies.

White-tailed deer sometimes live together

As summer melts into fall, the does become less territorial and may associate with nearby females and their fawns, which gives the young deer experience with other families. Since young does tend to set up territories next to those of their mother, chances are that nearby deer are close relatives. Later on, as the deer move farther and farther from their fawning territories and food becomes less abundant, does can get quite aggressive toward strangers. Does may do battle, chasing and striking at one another with their sharp hooves. Fawns learn such aggressive behavior from their mothers and begin threatening other fawns.

Bucks lose their shiny summer fur and grow their thicker, grayer winter coats first, sometimes as early as late August. The does and fawns molt later. Fawns keep their spotted coats for about three and a half months. During the

in small groups of related does and fawns.

winter, food is sometimes hard to find. Deer that have found the best summer food supply are the most likely to survive. Fawns are especially at risk of starvation. In the Adirondacks, most fawns die if winter (more than fifteen inches of snow on the ground) lasts more than 80 days. Well-fed adults, on the other hand, can make it through 120 days of winter.

When spring arrives, plants send out new shoots that nourish the hungry deer. The surviving fawns tend to stay in familiar territory. So do young does. But after two or three winters, most young bucks wander away, leaving their relatives behind. When they find another group of female deer, they settle down. In the late fall, the bucks accompany the other deer to their winter range. From then on, that area will be their home.

Chapter Three

Mule Deer

The mule deer *(Odocoileus hemionus)* is named for its mule-like large ears. Also called muleys, these animals are generally larger than whitetails. Muley bucks can weigh close to 400 pounds (180 kilograms); only the northernmost whitetails get this large. A muley's narrow tail is white, like the rump patch, except for its black tip. In parts of its range, the mule deer is dubbed the black-tailed deer, for the entire outer surface of the tail is black, not just the tip.

Mule and black-tailed deer live mostly in northwestern America, although their range extends southward into Baja California and other parts of northern Mexico. Muleys range eastward into Alberta, Saskatchewan, the Dakotas, Nebraska, Kansas, the Oklahoma panhandle, and parts of

Mule deer doe and fawn.

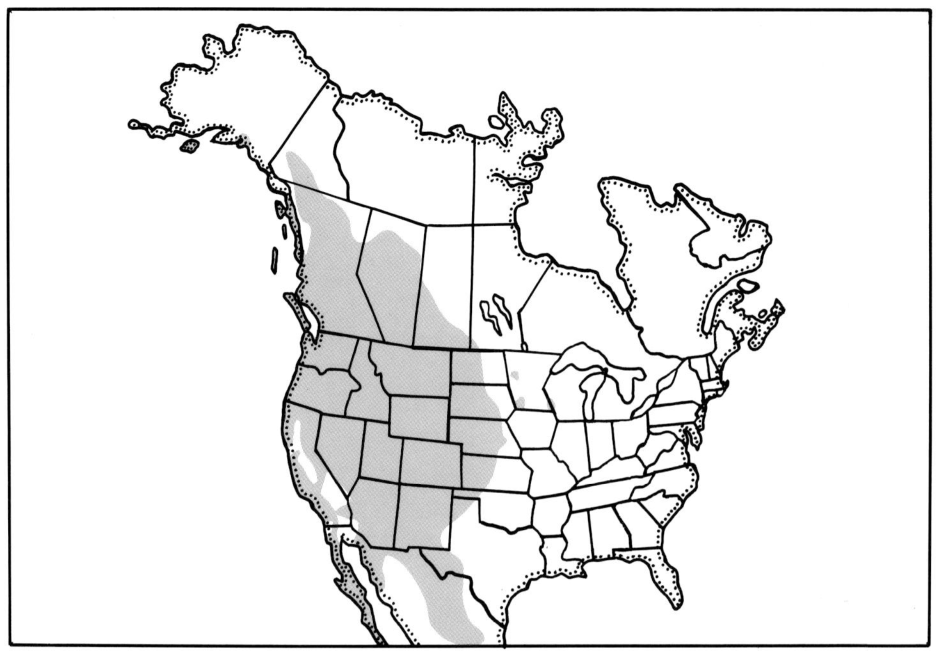

Mule deer distribution.

northern Texas. They range farther north than whitetails, living in parts of the Yukon Territory. The Sitka black-tailed deer inhabits coastal Alaska, while the Columbian blacktail is found along the Pacific coast from northern British Columbia south into California.

Mule Deer or Whitetail?

In regions like the Mountain West, where both mule deer and whitetails live, it helps to know how to tell the two apart. Mule deer are larger and have bigger ears. But when only one kind of deer is in view, these differences may not be obvious.

The easiest way to identify deer is to watch as they retreat. While running away, mule deer keep their tails down. Their white rump patches show clearly, but mule deer don't raise and flag their tails as whitetails do. Their gait also differs. Whitetails run with a smooth canter or gallop, sometimes leaping between strides. Mule deer, however, have a stiff-legged gait and may bound along, springing on all fours at one time. This gait allows them to zigzag unpredictably up the rough slopes of the mountainside habitat they often favor.

The antlers of the two species are also distinct. Each of the whitetail's antlers has a main beam that curves forward.

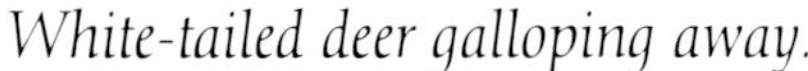

White-tailed deer galloping away.

Developing whitetail antlers, showing single points.

As the buck gets older, new single points grow directly off the main beams when new antlers grow each year. Muley antlers also have two main beams, but each beam forks into two smaller ones. In older bucks, each of these beams forks again so that mule deer bucks average four tines per side. Near the base of the antlers, a single small point also grows, as with whitetails. In both species, however, bucks with unusual branching patterns exist. Instead of just one small point growing from the main beams, for example, a muley buck may have two small tines on one side and just one on the other.

Mule deer buck, showing forked antlers.

Mule deer and whitetails are closely related and can interbreed, so their life cycles are quite similar. But there are differences. Muleys are often found in the same kinds of places as whitetails, especially where forests meet meadows and mountains approach the plains. But they prefer a more rugged habitat and live at higher altitudes into the Rocky Mountains. Muleys also inhabit western deserts where whitetails are absent. During the year, muleys move around more than whitetails. In the summer, they may migrate to high elevations, returning to valleys and sage flats during the winter.

Mule deer are more sociable and live in more open country than whitetails. They are also less shy, except where they are extensively hunted. While whitetails will usually spook and run at the sight of people, mule deer more easily become used to human presence and may show up at midday to munch on someone's carefully tended flower bed or ivy patch. When yelled at, the muleys may raise their heads, huge ears pointed toward the sound, and just stand there, retreating only reluctantly.

Mule deer often live in rough country.

Muleys spend more time in the open than do whitetails.

Chapter Four

Elk

A small group of cow elk hurriedly crosses the road at Mammoth Hot Springs in Yellowstone National Park as several cars pull over to the side of the road. A magnificent bull elk comes along just behind the cows. He pauses, lowers his neck, then points his nose upward. The bull lets out a strange, high-pitched squeal that slides up the scale, briefly holds a high note, then descends. The eerie sound seems to echo from the nearby hillside — but no. There on the ridge line stalks another bull, answering the first with his own unearthly bugling.

The cows stop in their tracks and look toward the far-off second bull, ears pricked in his direction. The first bull

Bull elk bugling.

Elk bulls spar to determine which is strongest.

bugles again, and the second responds as he slowly approaches along the ridge. Then the first bull attacks a sagebrush bush with his antlers, digging into the dirt in front of the bush and brushing its branches roughly. The rival elk comes closer until he reaches a bend in the trail. He stops, then turns to the right, walking away from the first bull and the cows. He isn't going to challenge a bigger, stronger, healthier animal. The cows turn away and begin to graze, and the first bull joins them. For now, they are still his.

Elk — A Different Story

White-tailed and mule deer are sociable only at certain times of the year, and the bucks normally deal with only one doe at a time. Elk, on the other hand, are basically social animals, with a herd structure that persists almost year round. During the fall breeding season, bull elk compete for possession of harem groups of up to twenty cows that stay with them for a number of days. Around the middle of October, mating is finished, and the males leave to form their own groups.

During the winter, elk may gather in herds of as many as a thousand animals. When spring arrives, pregnant females leave the groups. An elk cow gives birth to a single calf

Part of an elk herd grazing.

weighing 30 to 45 pounds (14 to 20 kilograms) in late May or early June. Twins are rare. The cows live separately with their new calves for several weeks. As spring turns to summer, the elk gradually congregate until herds of up to four hundred animals have formed. The herds are led by older cows and consist of cows with calves and young cows and bulls. When they are two or three years old, the young bulls join small groups of mature males that live apart from the herds.

A cow and her very young calf.

The young calf nurses.

An elk cow.

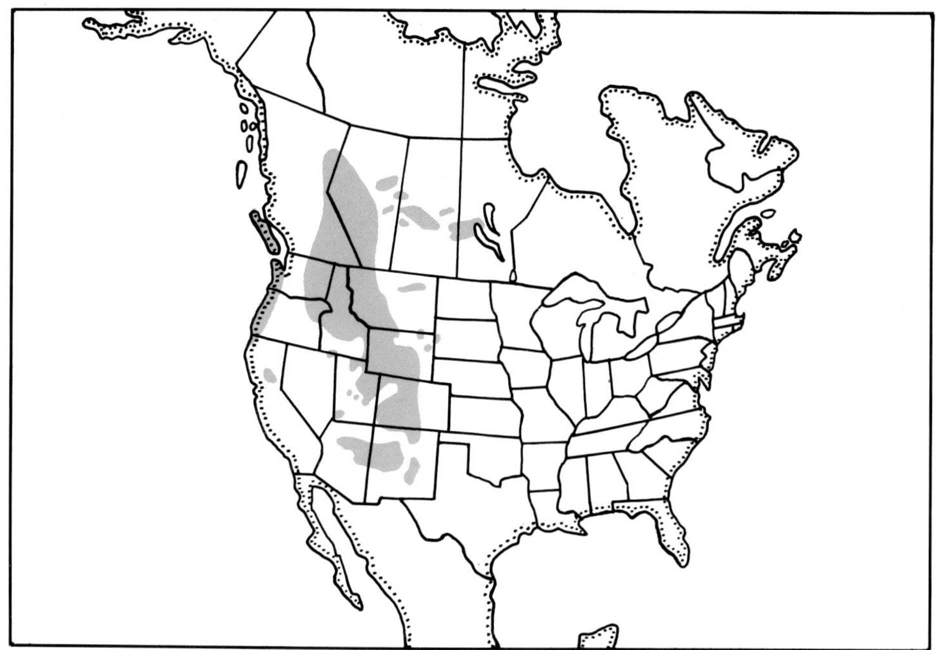

Elk distribution.

The Successful Elk

The animal we call elk is known to scientists as *Cervus elaphus*. This species lives across the northern parts of Asia, Europe, and North America. While the name most familiar to us is elk, some people prefer the Native American name, wapiti, to avoid confusion; in Europe the name elk is used for what we call moose! In Europe, *Cervus elaphus* is referred to as the "red deer."

Elk are much larger than mule deer, with bulls almost 5 feet (1.5 meters) tall at the shoulder. Bulls can weigh up to

1,100 pounds (almost 500 kilograms). The average bull weighs almost 800 pounds (364 kilograms), while cows average 600 pounds (273 kilograms). In the entire deer family, only moose are bigger than elk.

Elk have rich reddish brown coats. The body coat is lighter in color than that of the head and legs. The winter coat is more gray, with darker head and legs. Elk have somewhat longer fur around their necks, making a mane that is more noticeable in winter than summer. The calves are reddish brown with spots that last until early fall. All elk have a large, buffy rump patch and a small tail.

Four varieties of elk survive in North America. The most familiar is the Rocky Mountain elk that ranges through the Rocky Mountain states. The elk in Yellowstone National Park are this type, with large bodies and impressive antlers. The Manitoban elk of Saskatchewan and Manitoba is bigger but has smaller antlers, while the Roosevelt's elk of Oregon and Washington is even bigger, but with modest antlers. The rare tule elk of central and northern California is the smallest type. The tule elk is still big, though, with bulls averaging 550 pounds (250 kilograms).

Elk are primarily grazers, spending most of their time feeding in open meadows. Elk are the most vocal of our cervids. Because elk are social animals, communication is important to them, and a herd of cows and calves can set up quite a racket of modest bugles, barklike warnings, whistles, and catlike meows.

Elk are very sensitive to human presence and need large areas to survive. They often migrate many miles to reach their winter range. Before Europeans came to North America, the thousands of elk that spent the summers in the Rocky Mountains within what is now Grand Teton National Park, the south end of what is now Yellowstone National Park, and national forests to the east migrated down into the Jackson Hole Valley for the winter.

Jackson Hole is a spectacularly beautiful area south of Grand Teton National Park, prime real estate for people. The town of Jackson and surrounding development have blocked the migration route of the elk, and ranches occupy most of the elk's former winter range. To provide for the animals' needs in winter, the National Elk Refuge was established in 1911 at the north end of the valley and was fenced at the southern end, preventing the elk from completing their migration. Instead, 7,500 or more elk congregate on the 24,000-acre refuge for about six months each winter. During the harshest two and a half months, the animals are fed alfalfa pellets every day. Tourists can visit the refuge, riding horse-drawn sleighs out among the elk, which have become accustomed to the presence of people. When spring arrives, the elk migrate back north and spread out again into the mountains, becoming wild and independent creatures once more. The next winter they will again be dependent on human goodwill for their survival.

Elk on the National Elk Refuge.

Chapter Five

Deer and Elk in Today's World

The cervids of modern-day North America live in a give-and-take with human beings. Deer and elk once lived in harmony with Native American inhabitants. Indians hunted the animals for their delicious meat and useful hides and antlers, and may have helped keep their populations in check. But the animals remained abundant. Settlers, however, hunted deer extensively, often slaughtering large numbers so their meat and hides could be sold. Even in colonial times, laws had to be passed in some areas to protect deer from being overhunted. By the beginning of the twentieth century, both the once-abundant whitetails and

Before Europeans came to North America, there was plenty of space for animals such as deer.

the mule deer had been eliminated from most of their range. The estimated 23 to 40 million whitetails had been reduced to between 300,000 to 500,000 individuals, while the 5 to 13 million mule deer had dropped to about the same numbers as the whitetails. Meanwhile, elk were exterminated in eastern and central North America as well as in the southwestern United States and Mexico. Populations in Canada and the western United States had also dropped drastically.

Fortunately, conservation measures saved all three species. Market hunting was replaced by carefully regulated hunting seasons that allowed populations to increase. Today, whitetails are abundant in many areas, with a total population of around 20 million. In some areas, especially where logging has created the patchwork terrain that whitetails prefer, more deer live than before. Mule deer reached high numbers during the 1960s. But as the human population of the West increased, mule deer habitat disappeared, and mule deer populations continue to decline. Scientists estimate that there are now around 5.5 million mule deer. There may be as many as a million elk in North America today, thanks to legal protection.

Controlling Deer and Elk Populations

The controversy over whether animals like deer and elk should be hunted has become very intense. On one side are those who believe people shouldn't kill other living things.

On the other are hunters and many wildlife managers, who see value in hunting.

Hunting advocates point out that by eliminating wolves in most of the United States, humans have taken away the major predator of deer and elk. Of all the original predators on cervids in North America, only coyotes, black bears, and humans are common now. Deer populations are more dense than before — deer like the patchy habitat of alternating woods and open spaces humans create, and now they have fewer predators. In addition, most of their former habitat has been taken over by people, forcing the deer into smaller and smaller areas. Such dense populations can cause a number of problems for both humans and natural environments. For example, mountain lions, another deer predator, follow their prey and can become a problem for people in areas where deer have become abundant.

Populations of deer — especially whitetail — have exploded to the point where the animals are destroying their own habitat. When deer overpopulate, they threaten the survival of plant life. Wildflowers such as trillium disappear from the forest floor. Tree seedlings are eaten, removing the young trees that would have grown to replace old ones that die. Even older trees can be weakened when deer eat too many of their branches. Yet when wildlife managers propose eliminating some deer through hunting to bring back the natural balance, citizens often object loudly.

Deer populations must be controlled where they have

gotten out of hand. Leaving the situation alone to "let nature take its course" is no solution. After upsetting the ecological balance of their environment through overfeeding, the deer themselves suffer from massive starvation, as did the elk in Yellowstone National Park in 1989. Hunting is not allowed in national parks. But if wolves are brought back into Yellowstone, they will help keep elk populations from exploding if a series of mild winters comes along.

Overpopulation of deer causes problems for people as well as for nature. Pennsylvania farmers lose about $30 million in crops to deer each year. The problem of crop losses is equally serious in many other states. Deer on the road are a serious traffic hazard — in just one state (Illinois) in 1989, there were 12,152 reported deer-vehicle accidents, resulting in 450 human injuries and four deaths. Around the country, about a hundred people and a quarter of a million deer die this way every year.

Deer also spread Lyme disease, a very painful infection that can cause crippling arthritis or even death. People get the disease from a tiny tick that infests deer and mice. In areas where the deer population has exploded, the incidence of Lyme disease has also grown. The number of Lyme disease cases in Westchester County, New York, for example, grew from 1,419 in 1988 to 2,657 in 1990, as the deer population set new records.

Many people don't like the idea of shooting deer to reduce their populations. But other methods are generally

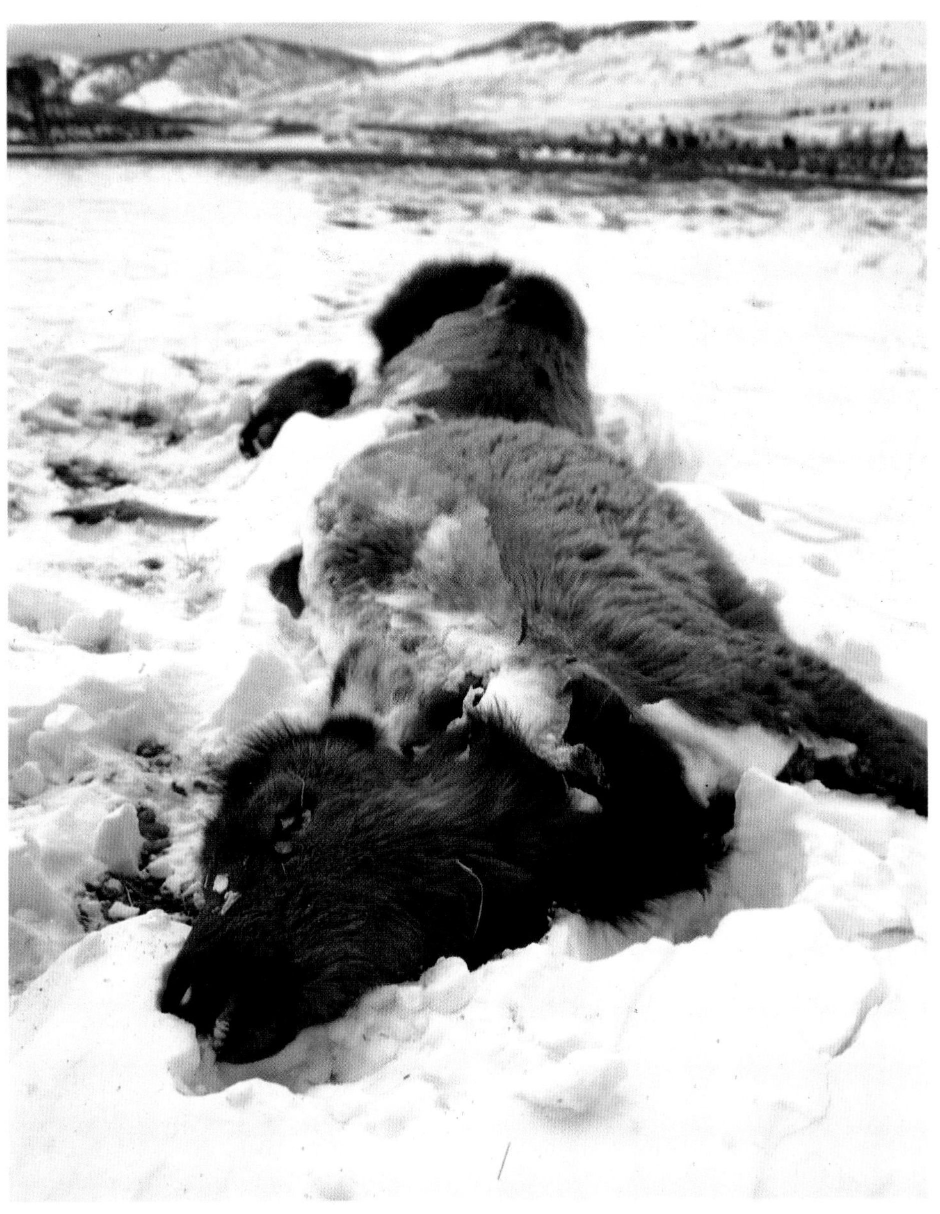

This elk is one of hundreds to die in Yellowstone National Park after the hard winter of 1989.

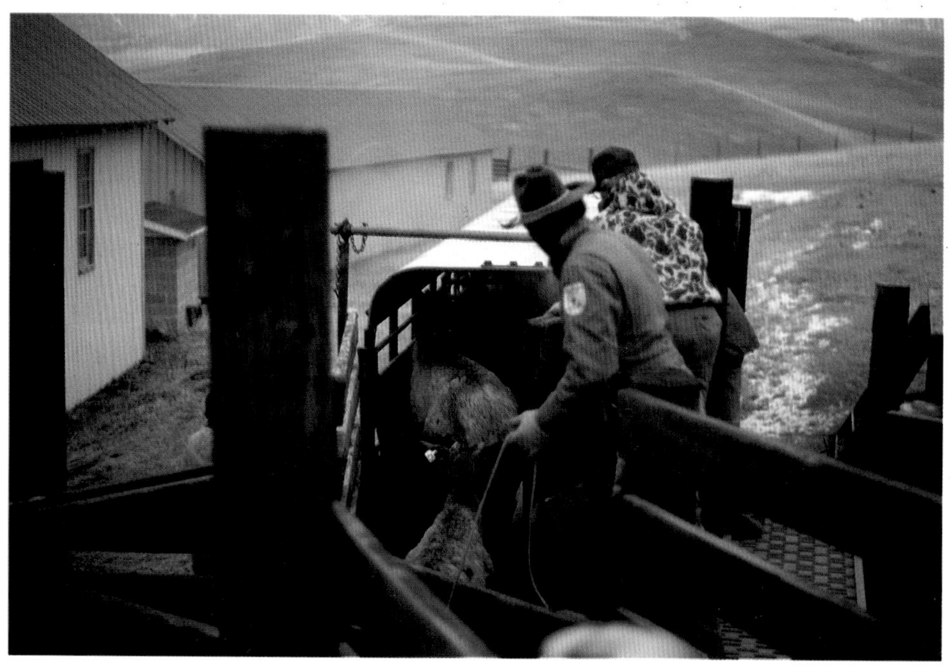

Unlike deer, when elk overpopulate, there is a good chance they will be wanted elsewhere. These excess elk from the National Bison Range are going to Iowa.

either impractical or too expensive. Trapping deer and moving them is not a good solution. First of all, it costs more than four hundred dollars per animal to trap and relocate deer. Secondly, there are few takers for excess deer — overpopulation is widespread. And lastly, deer don't usually do well after being moved. They have difficulty finding food in unfamiliar territory and may more easily stumble onto roads where they get hit by cars. When 15 of 215 black-tailed deer removed from Angel Island, California, were tracked by radio collars, it was discovered that only two survived in their new environment after one year.

Modern technology may help resolve the overpopulation problem in some areas. A new hormone shot that can be delivered by dart guns prevents fertilization and therefore the birth of fawns. But darting enough deer to have a significant effect on a large population is a difficult proposition. Even when applied to restricted populations, the hormone treatment is expensive. A pilot program proposed for the tule elk in California would cost $1,400 to treat just fifteen does the first year.

Where deer become overpopulated, shooting, either by hunters or by marksmen hired for the job, is still the most practical solution. The meat from the deer serves a good purpose, too. It is much leaner than beef, so it is healthier to eat. And when deer are removed by shooting, the meat can be distributed to schools and to kitchens that feed the hungry and homeless.

Preserving Habitat

Even though many places are plagued by too many deer, maintenance of habitat for both deer and elk is essential for their long-term survival. One reason, aside from lack of predators, why parks and preserves have too many deer is that the animals can't extend their territory to accommodate their numbers. A park or refuge may be completely surrounded by private land where deer aren't welcome.

Bosque del Apache National Wildlife Refuge in New Mexico was set aside for cranes, but these mule deer benefit from the refuge, too.

Cervids have different needs in summer and winter, so they require different habitats at these times. In mountainous regions, all three species move to lower elevations during the wintertime. They need the same type of habitat for winter survival as is favored by humans — low-elevation hillsides or valleys with flowing streams. When subdivisions of housing for humans take over such habitat, animals have no place to go and are more likely to starve. Mule deer and elk are especially sensitive to such loss of winter habitat.

At the end of winter, deer and elk often move to even lower elevations than they used during the winter, for there the first green foliage of springtime appears. Abundant spring food is especially critical for pregnant does and cows. In April, an elk fetus weighs just under five and a half pounds. Between then and birth in June, it needs to gain twenty-five pounds or more. This can happen only if the mother eats plenty of nourishing, protein-rich greenery.

These whitetails are taking advantage of the greening up of a low, wet meadow in early spring.

Tourists in places like Yellowstone National Park are thrilled by the sight of a beautiful bull elk.

Protecting Wildlands

Maps may show many green areas representing public lands set aside for wildlife and for human recreation, but these areas are often chosen for their scenic beauty rather than for their ability to support wildlife year round. Outside of Alaska, at least 80 percent of our wildlife depends on private land for the food and cover required for survival. Most of this is agricultural land, and every year around a million acres of such farmland is lost to shopping centers, resorts, and residential development.

If we want to continue to share the earth with wildlife such as deer and elk, we need to plan carefully how we use our lands. People and wildlife can exist together. But we need to make sure we provide the habitats wild animals need for year-round survival. Then we will know that future generations will enjoy the grace and beauty of animals such as deer and elk as we do.

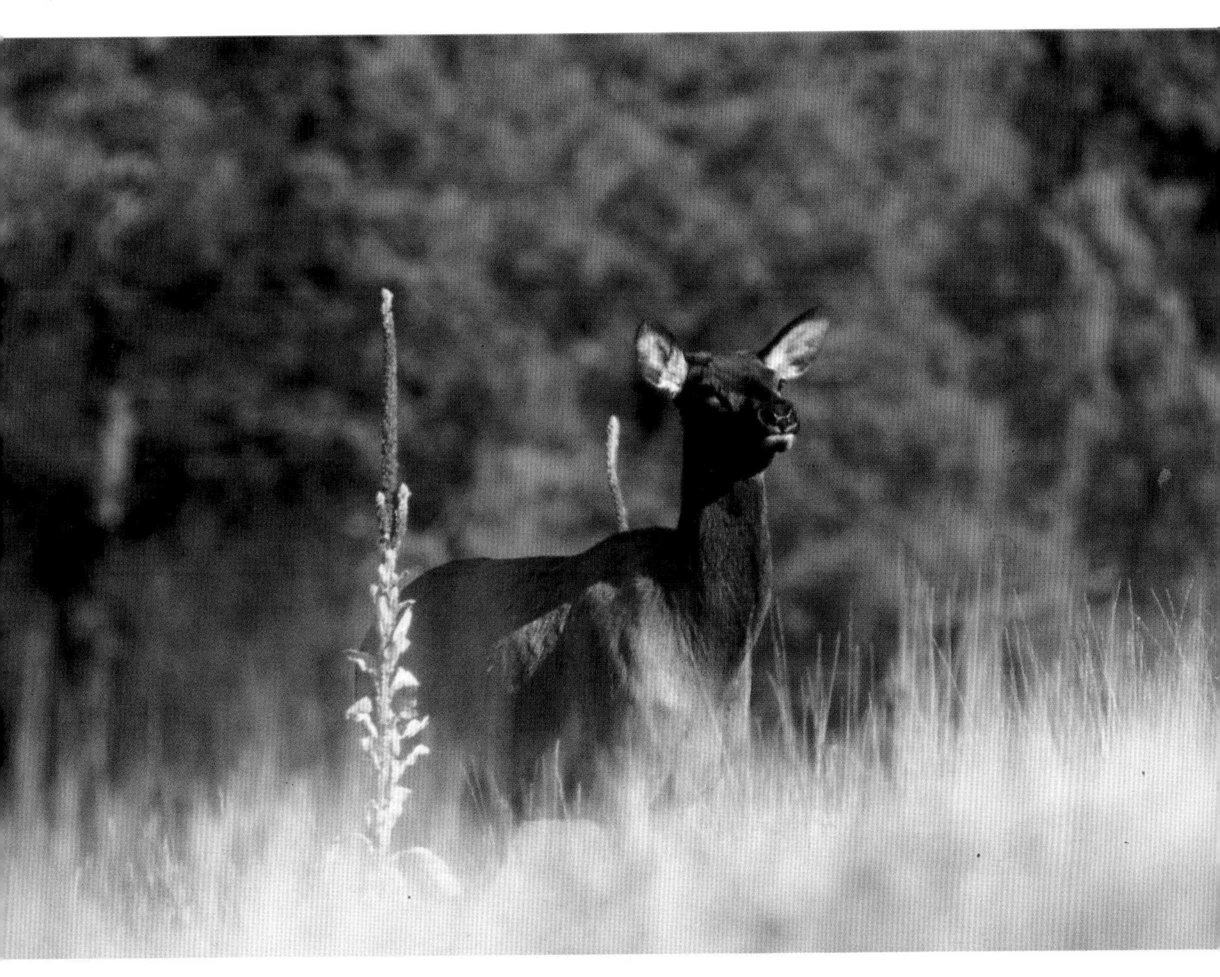

An older elk calf.

A bull elk in fall.

Selected Bibliography

This list contains some of the references consulted during work on this book. Students will find the starred (*) references particularly helpful.

*Barrett, Todd. "Oh, Deer!" *National Wildlife* 29 (1991): 16–21.

*Cox, Daniel J. *Elk.* San Francisco, CA: Chronicle Books, 1992.

*Geist, V. "Downtown Deer." *Natural History* 89 (1980): 56–64.

Henderson, Robert E., and Amy O'Herren. "Winter Ranges for Elk and Deer: Victims of Uncontrolled Subdivisions?" *Western Wildlands* (Spring 1992): 20–25.

*McKee, Russell. "Peregrinations and Permutations of a Contrary Eight-Toed Beast." *Audubon* 89 (1987): 52–80.

*Mills, Judy. "New Look at a Deer Old Game." *National Wildlife* 28 (1990): 4–9.

Nowak, Ronald M. *Walker's Mammals of the World.* 5th ed. Baltimore, MD: The Johns Hopkins Press, 1991.

*Ozoga, John. *Whitetail Country.* Minocqua, WI: NorthWord Press, 1988.

*Peterson, David. *Racks.* San Bernardino, CA: Borgo Press, 1991.

*Porter, William F. "High-Fidelity Deer." *Natural History* 101 (1992): 48–49.

Putnam, Rory. *The Natural History of Deer.* Ithaca, NY: Comstock Publishing Associates, 1988.

*Smith, Bruce. "History of the American Wapiti." *Bugle* 7 (1990): 6–12.

Index

Yellowstone elk in winter.

ABOUT THE AUTHOR AND PHOTOGRAPHER

Dorothy Hinshaw Patent holds a Ph.D. in zoology from the University of California at Berkeley. She has written more than seventy books for children and young adults on wildlife and wildlife management, most recently *Prairie Dogs.* In 1987, Dr. Patent received the Eva L. Gordon Award for Children's Science Literature for the body of her work. She and her husband, Gregory Patent, have two grown sons. They live in Missoula, Montana.

William Muñoz earned his B.A. degree in history from the University of Montana. He has collaborated with Dorothy Hinshaw Patent on many successful photo essays, including *Prairie Dogs.* He lives with his wife, Sandy, and son, Sean, in St. Ignatius, Montana, where he divides his time between freelance photography and gardening.